HEELS

It's all about shoes

Adult Coloring Book

50 Illustrations

By : Mehwish Abbas

Website: www.mehwish.me

✉ Email: hi@mehwish.me

Instagram: instagram.com/mehwishabb

Twitter: twitter.com/mehwishabb

Facebook: facebook.com/mehwishabb1

This book belongs to:

Tips for coloring

Please put two sheets of paper behind the page you want to color.
This will prevent transfer of ink or indentation on the page next to the page
you're coloring.

In my experience pencil colors give the best result on the kind of paper
Amazon uses for self published books like this one.

Please visit www.mehwish.me to see video tutorials where I demonstrate
how to color these pages. You will also find free adult coloring pages on my
website and I plan to publish more often.

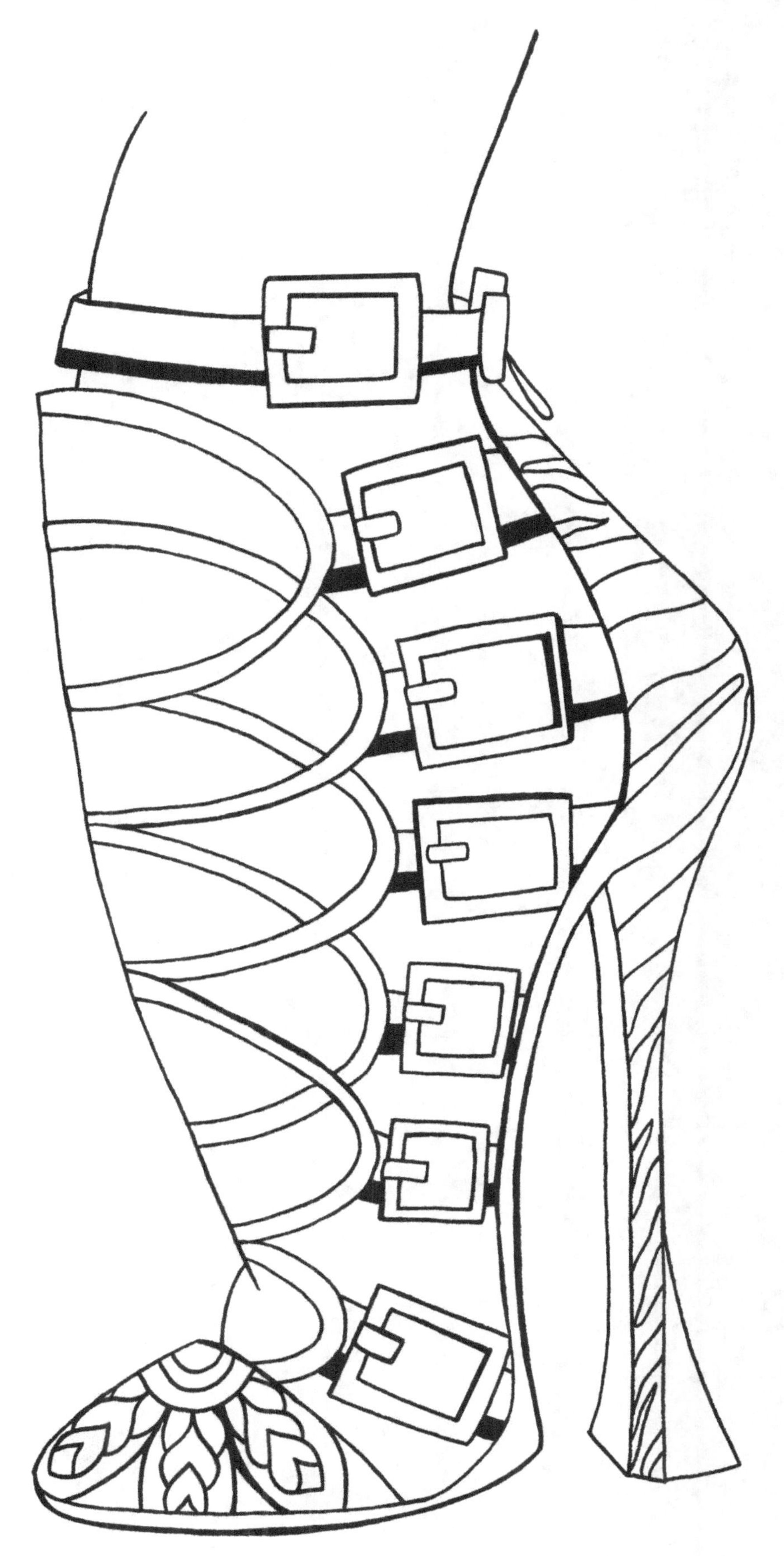

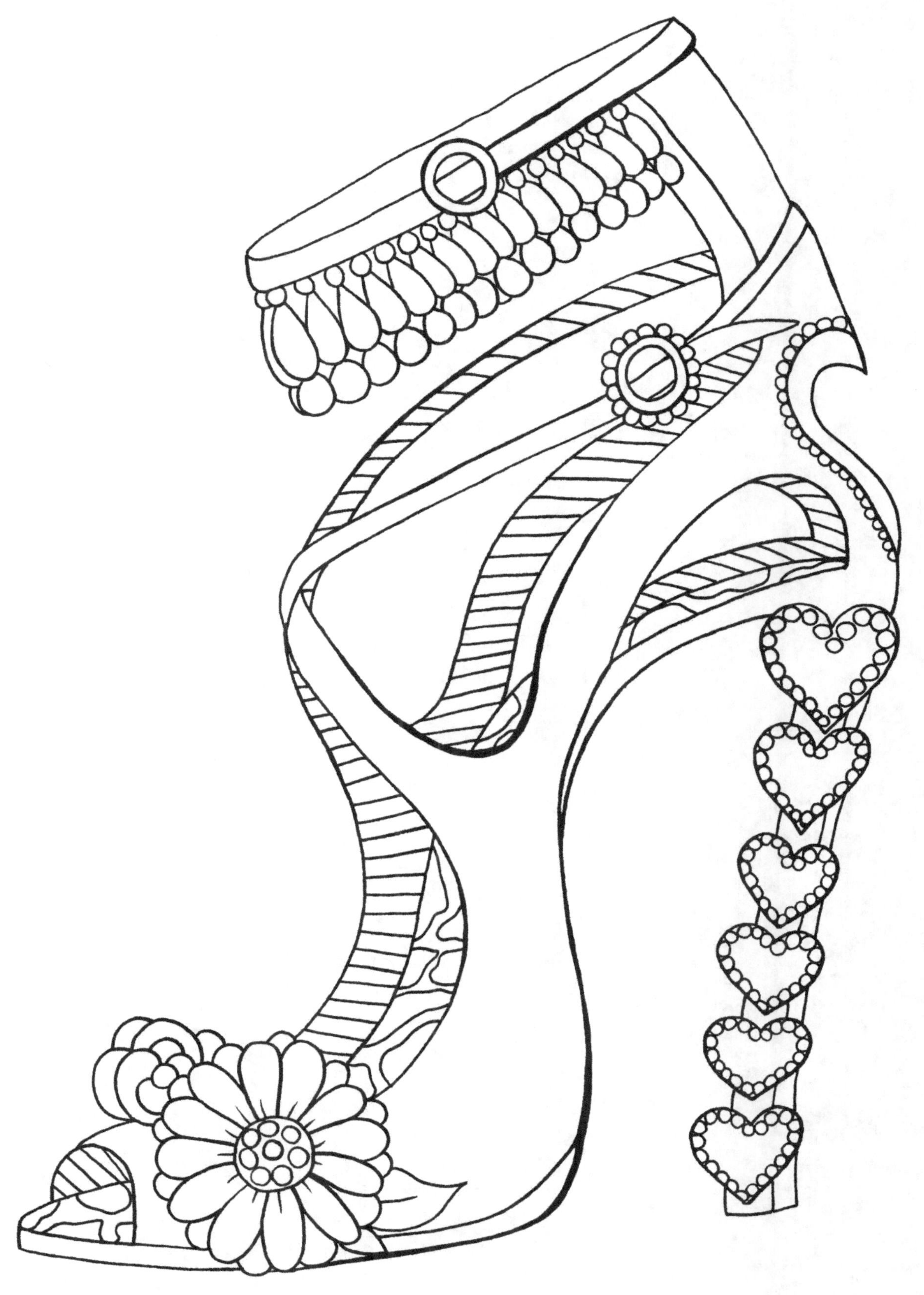

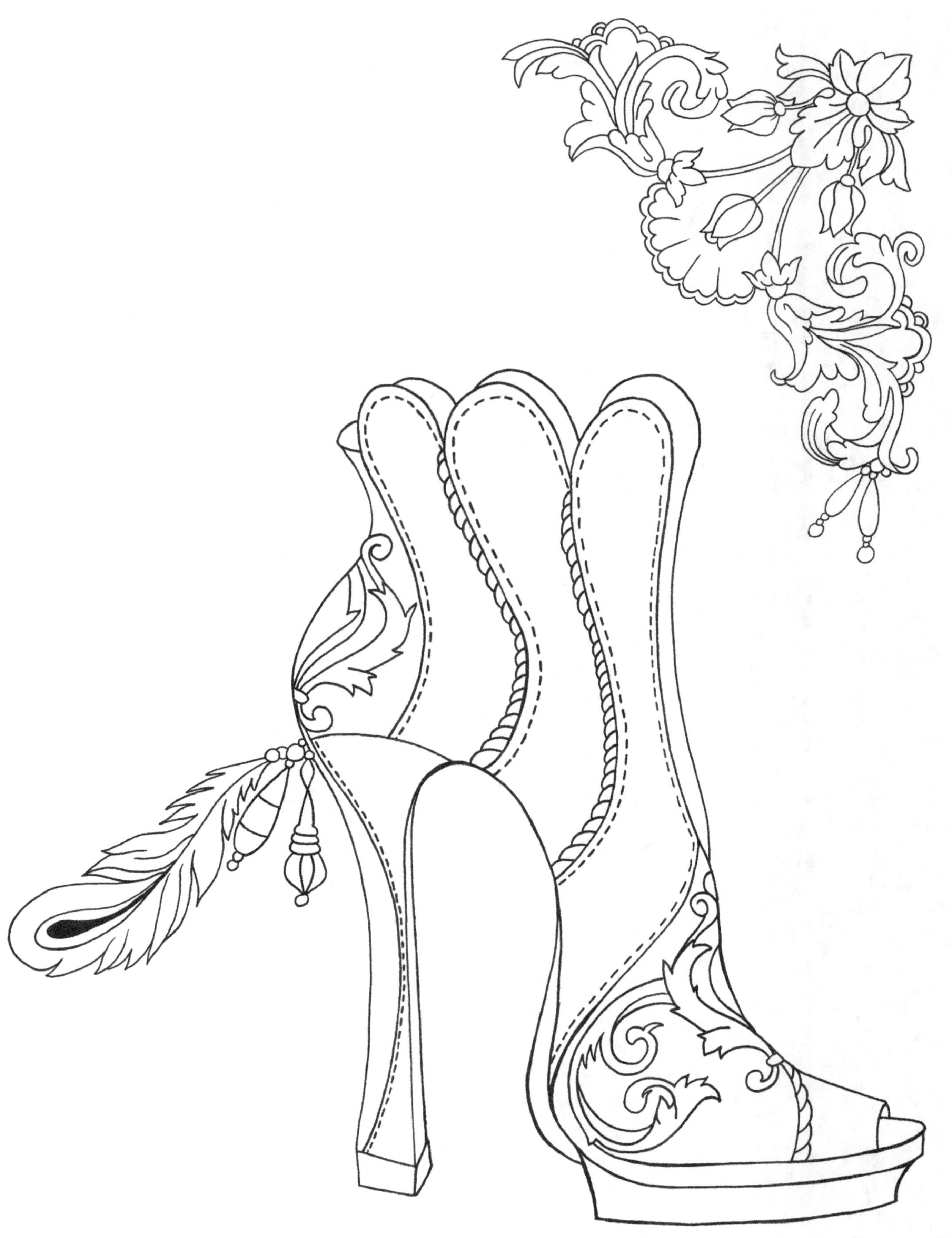

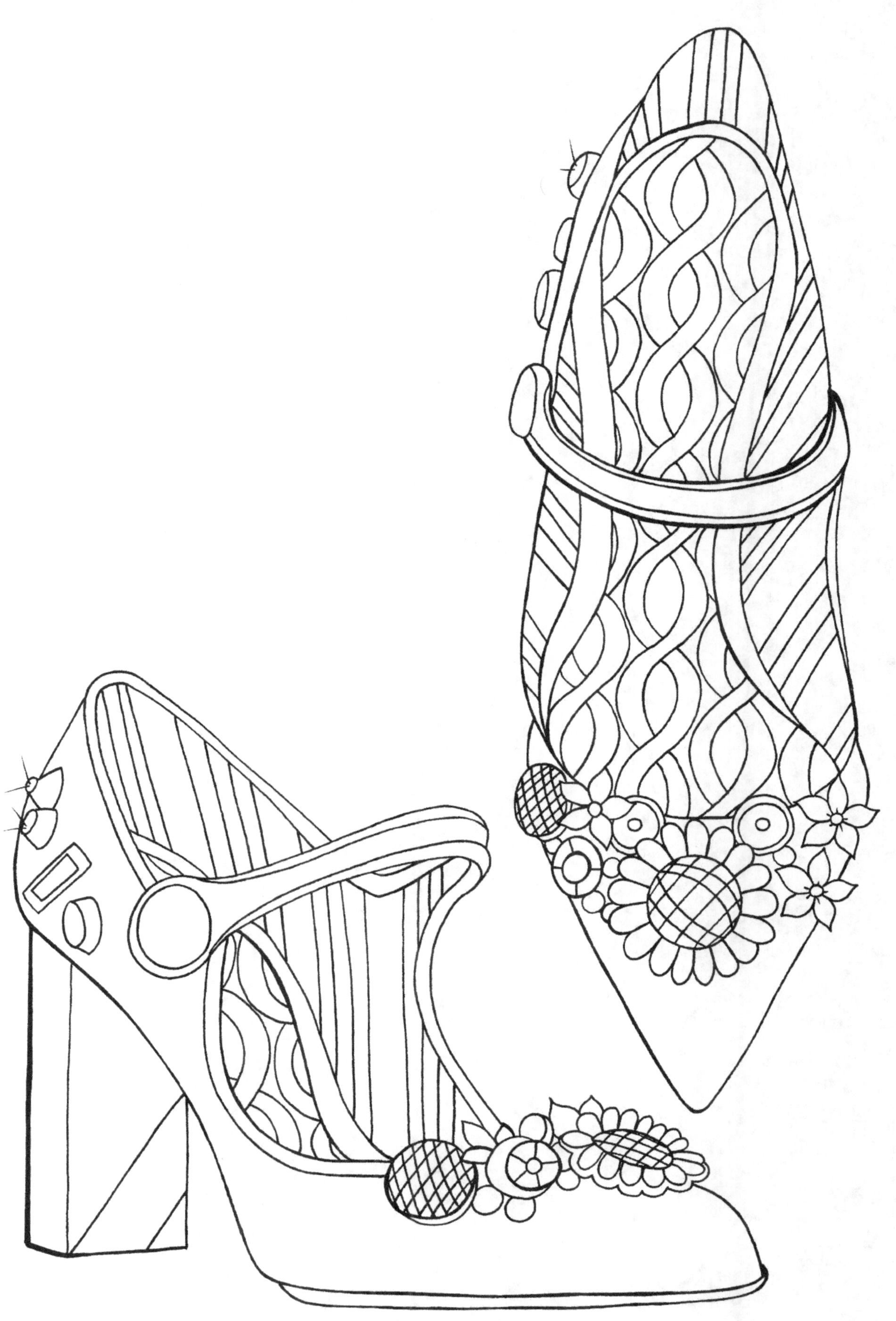

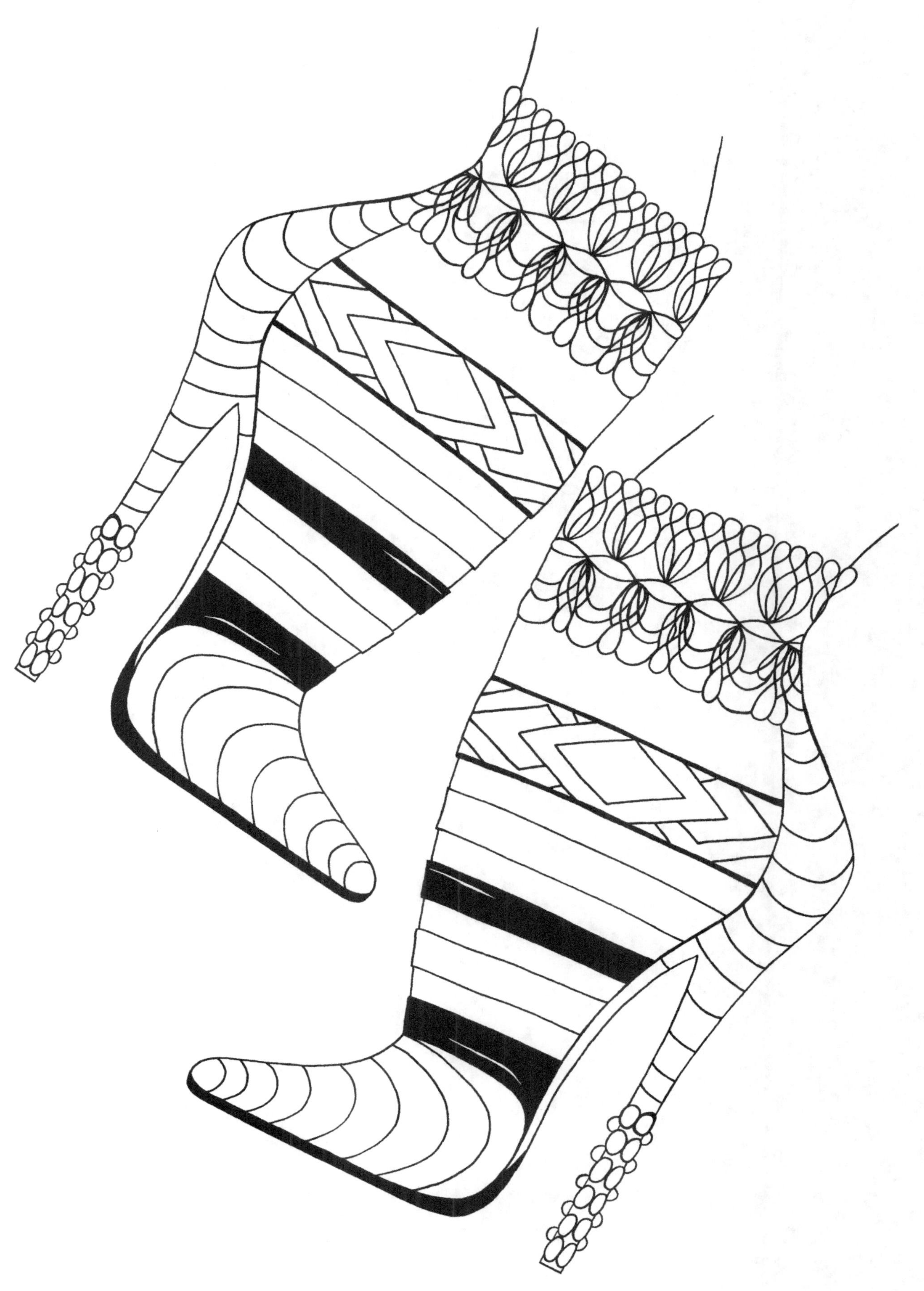

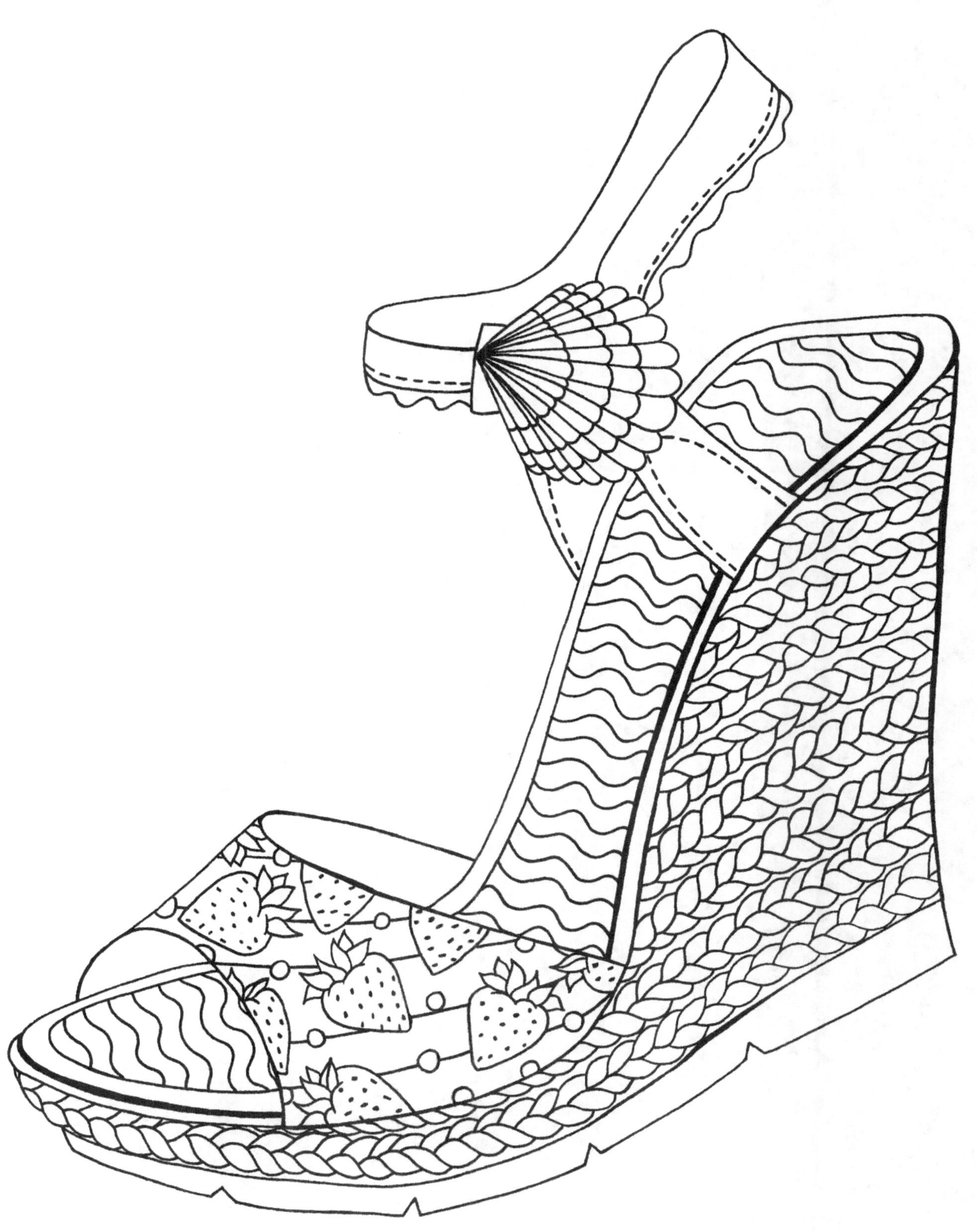

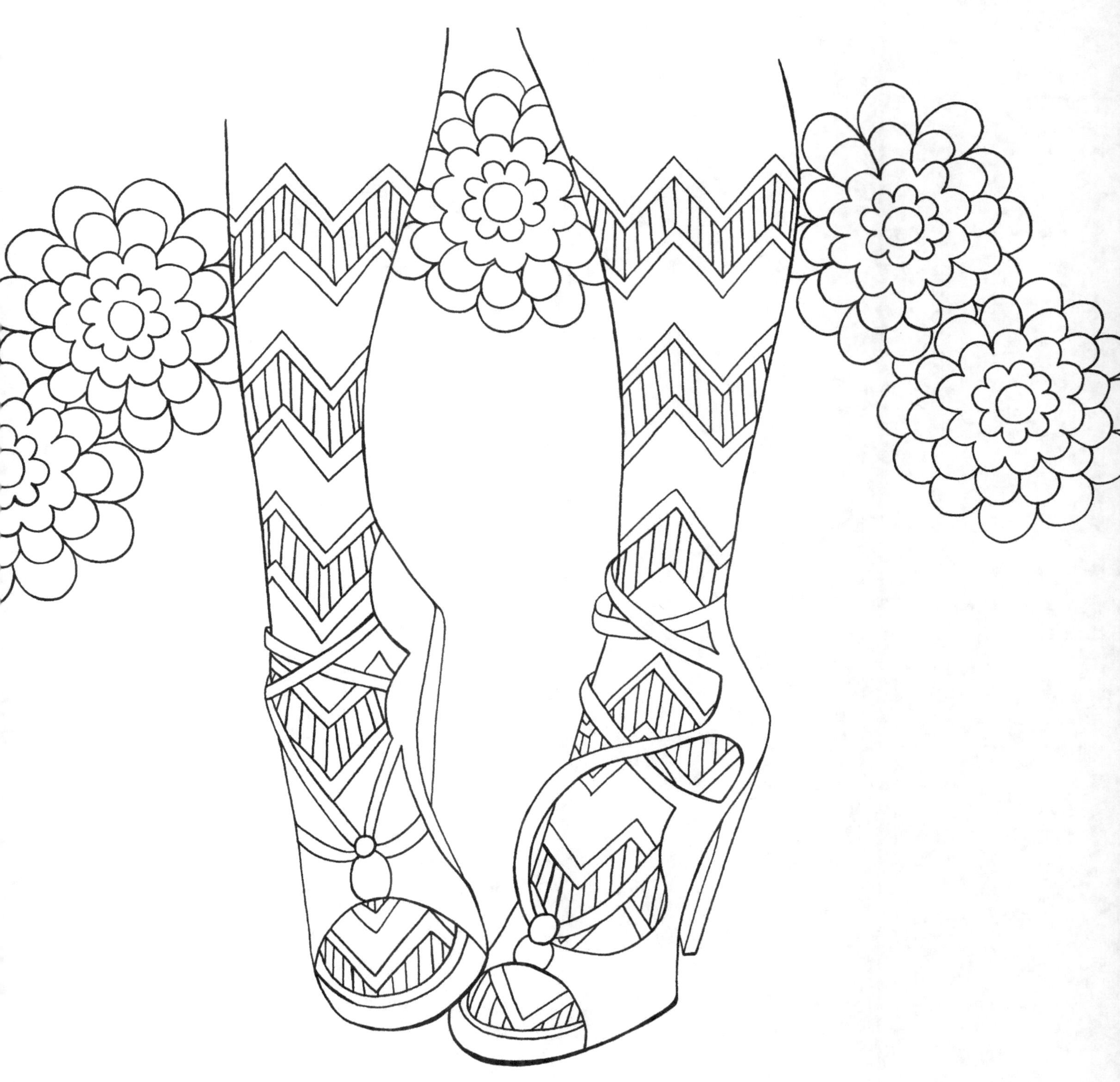

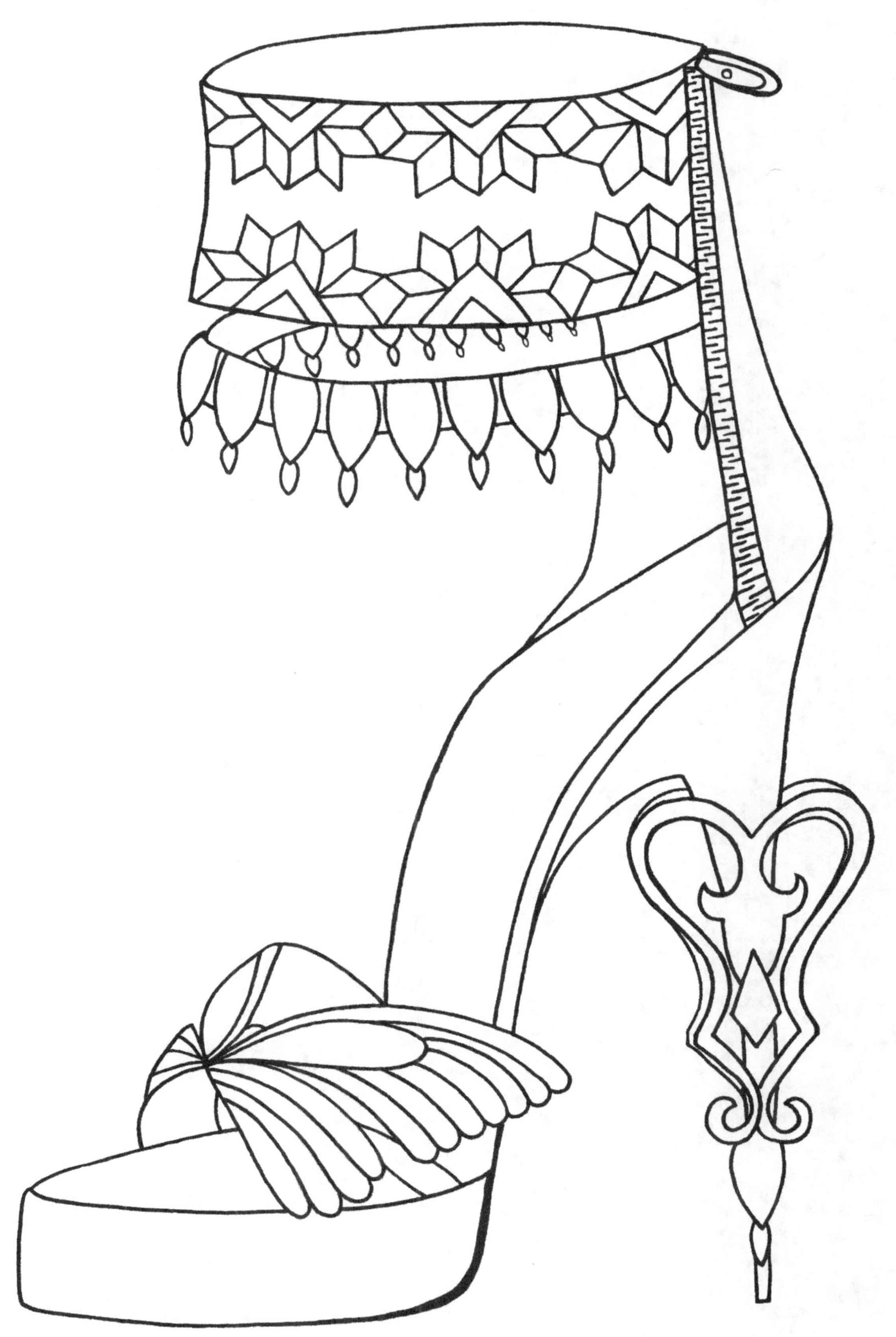

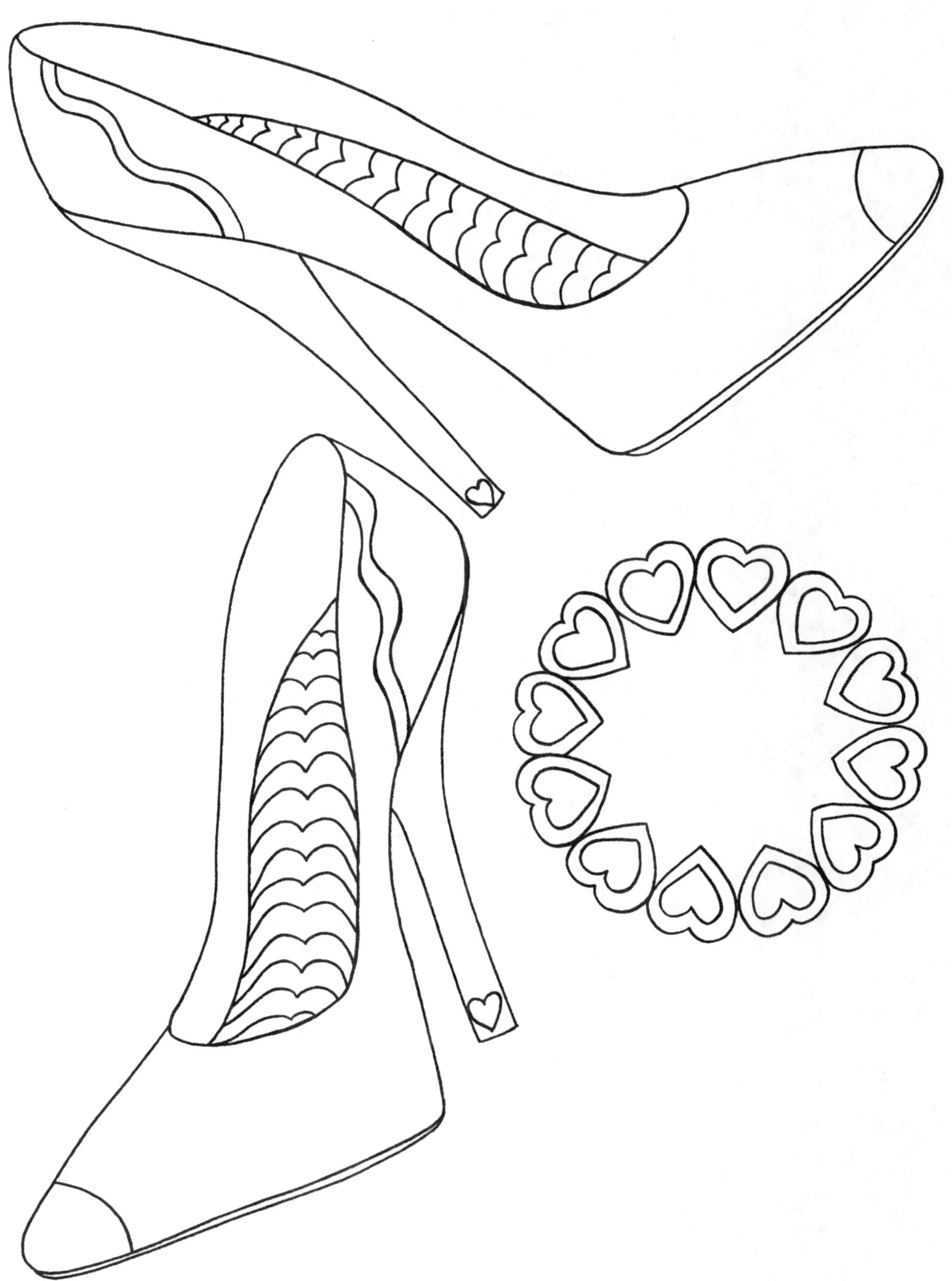

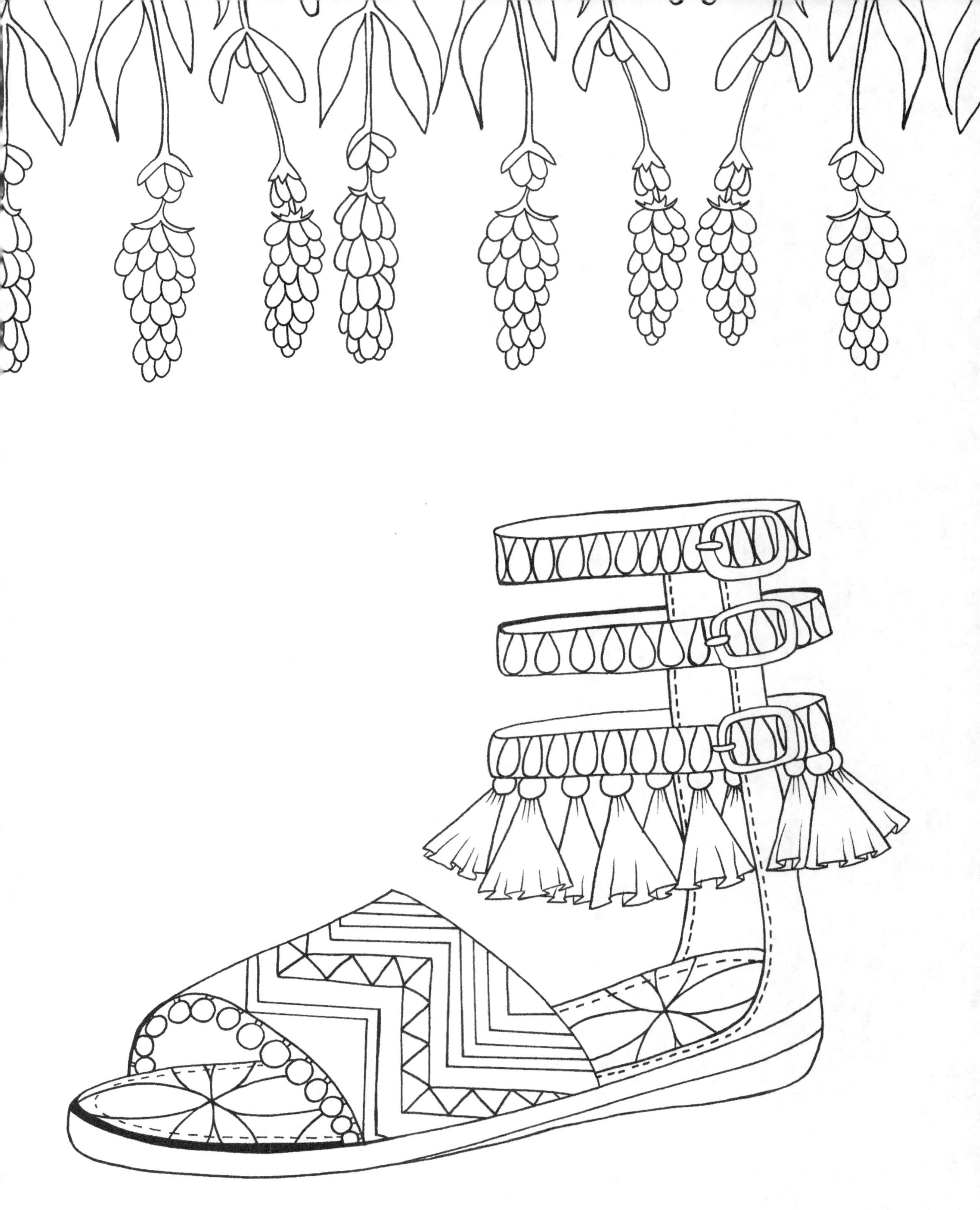

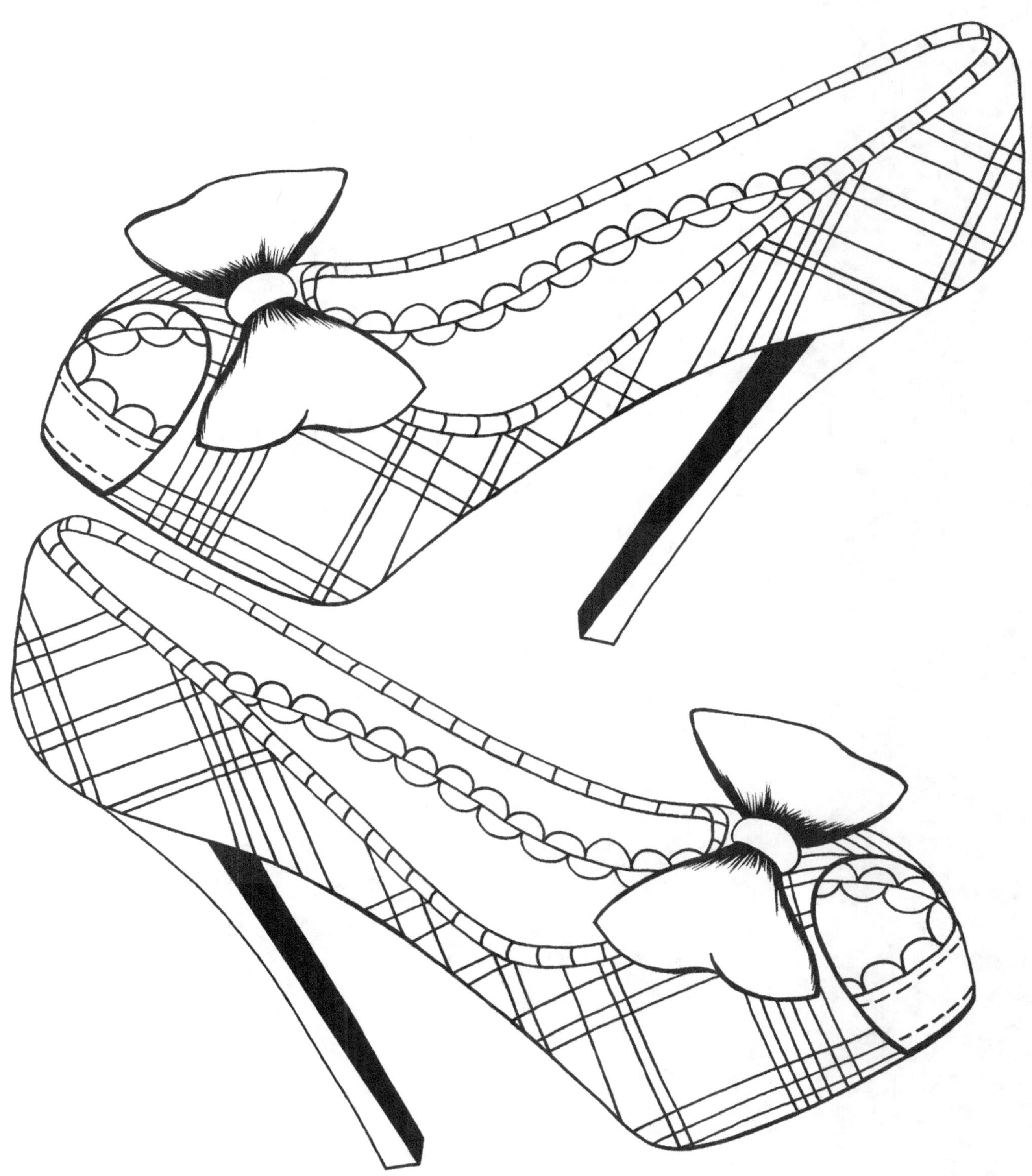

The end

I hope you had fun coloring this book.
If you want to get in touch or have feedback
please visit my Website: www.mehwish.me

✉ Email: hi@mehwish.me

Instagram: instagram.com/mehwishabb

Twitter: twitter.com/mehwishabb

Facebook: facebook.com/mehwishabb1

You can also checkout my other books.

Buy from Amazon. Thank you.

Color Palette Test Page